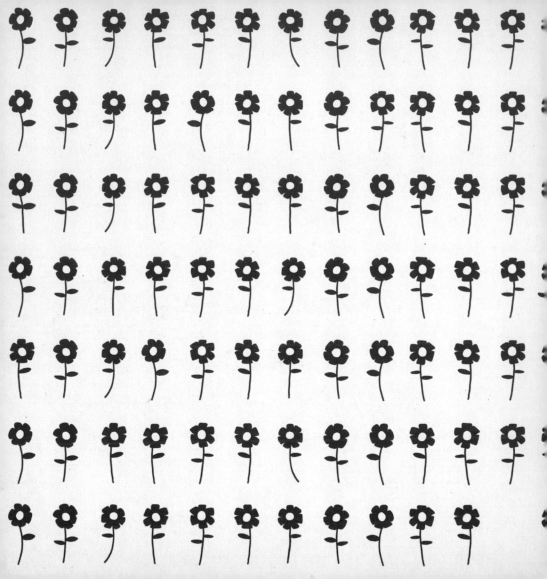

EXTREME OPPOSITES

BY MAX DALTON

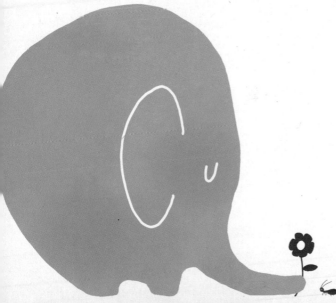

DAVID R. GODINE
Publisher · Boston

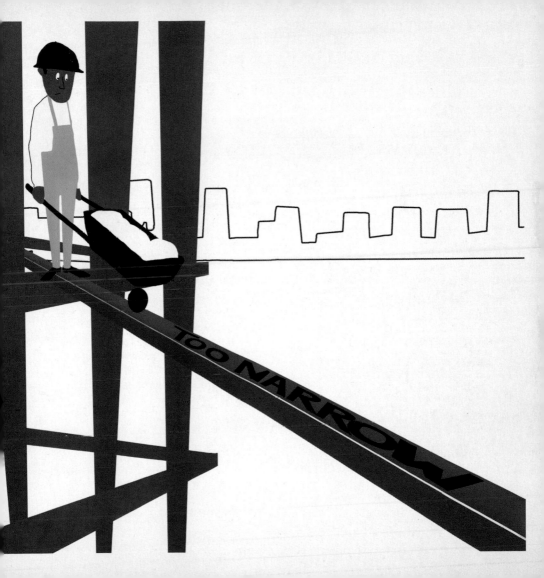

TOO
SOFT

TOO LIGHT

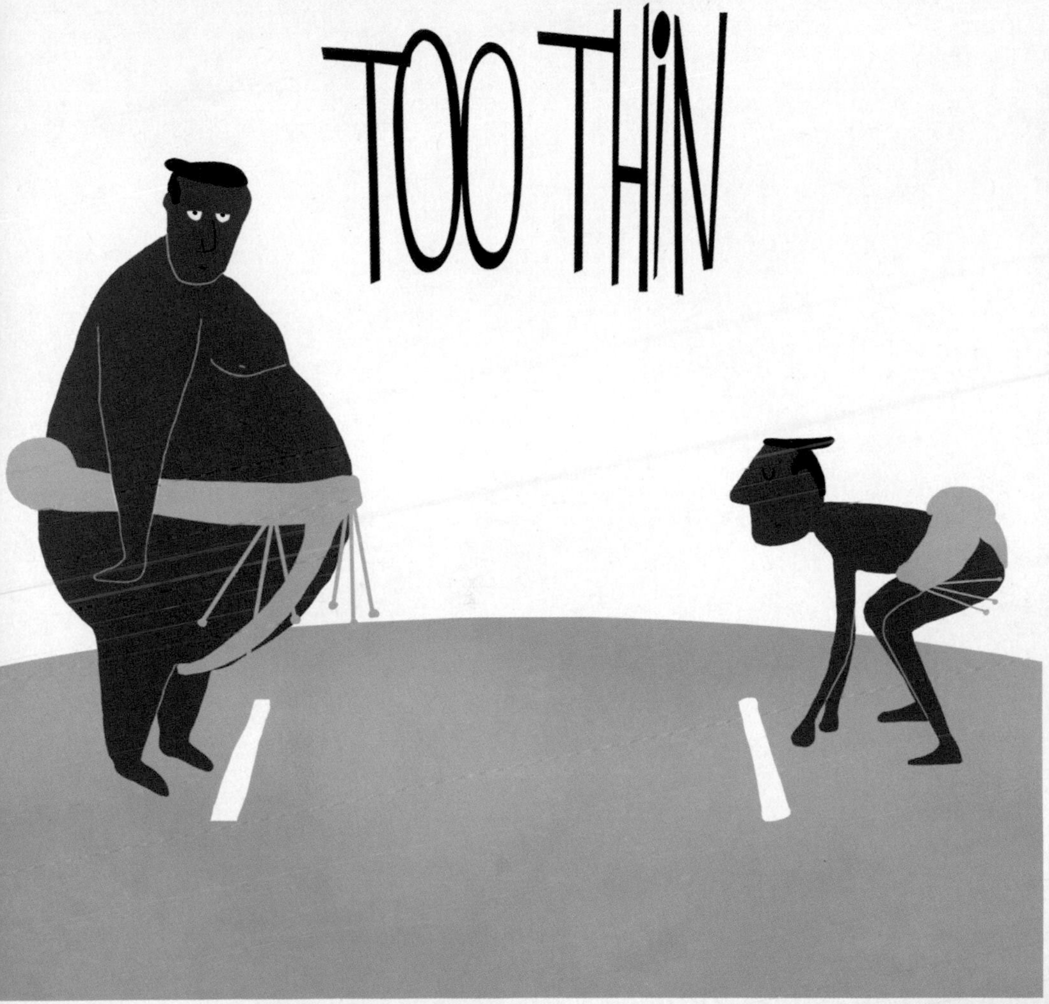
TOO THIN

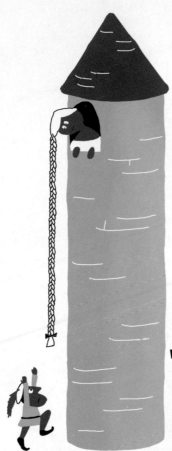

TOO SHORT

TOO WET

TOO
DARK

TOO
WEAK

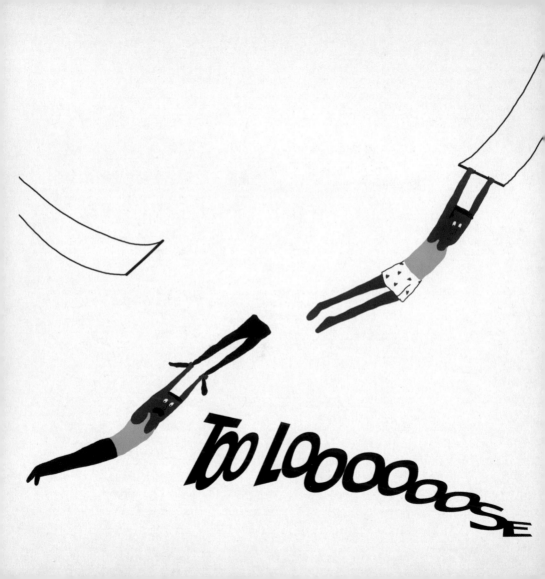

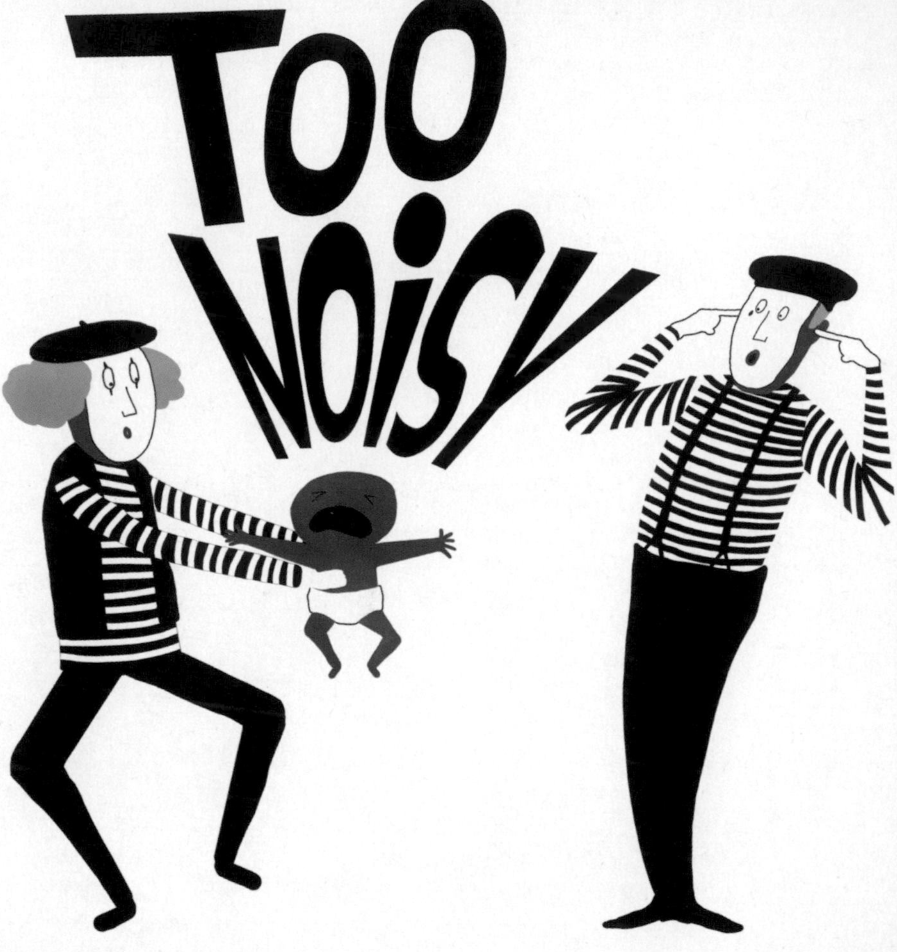
TOO
NOISY

THE END

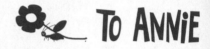

TO ANNIE

First published in 2013 by
DAVID R. GODINE, *Publisher*
Post Office Box 450
Jaffrey, New Hampshire 03452
www.godine.com

LIBRARY OF CONGRESS CATALOGING-IN-PUBLICATION DATA

Dalton, Max, author illustrator.
 Extreme opposites / Written and illustrated by Max Dalton.
    pages cm
ISBN 978-1-56792-503-6 (alk. paper)
1. English language—Synonyms and antonyms—Juvenile literature. I. Title.
 PE1591D217 2019
 428.1—dc23
2013010853

FIRST EDITION
Printed in China

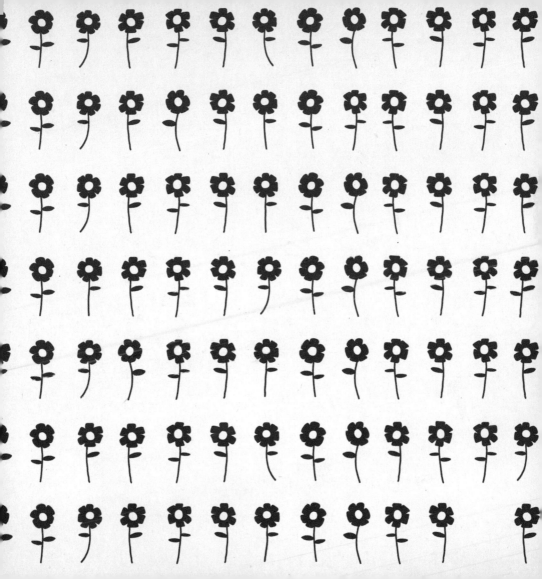

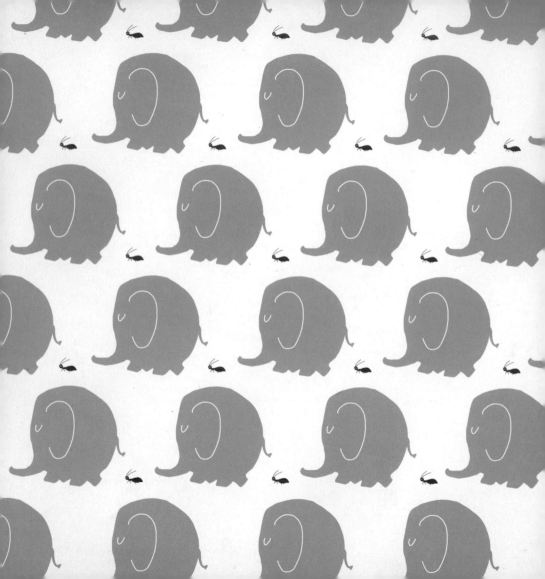